Pebble® Bilingüe/Bilingual Plus

Baila, baila, baila/Dance, Dance, Dance

Bailando tap/
Tap Dancing

por/by Kathryn Clay

Editora consultora/Consulting Editor: Gail Saunders-Smith, PhD

Asesora de contenido/Content Consultant: Heidi L. Schimpf
Directora de Programas y Servicios/Director of Programs and Services
Joy of Motion Dance Center, Washington, D.C.

CAPSTONE PRESS
a capstone imprint

Pebble Plus is published by Capstone Press,
151 Good Counsel Drive, P.O. Box 669, Mankato, Minnesota 56002.
www.capstonepub.com

Books published by Capstone Press are manufactured with paper
containing at least 10 percent post-consumer waste.

Library of Congress Cataloging-in-Publication Data
Clay, Kathryn.
  [Tap dancing. English & Spanish]
  Bailando tap / por Kathryn Clay = Tap Dancing / by Kathryn Clay.
  p. cm.—(Pebble Plus bilingüe/bilingual. Baila, baila, baila/Dance, dance, dance)
  Includes index.
  Summary: "Simple text and photographs present tap dancing, including
simple steps—in both English and Spanish"—Provided by publisher.
  ISBN 978-1-4296-5353-4 (library binding)
  1. Tap dancing—Juvenile literature. I. Title. II. Title: Tap dancing.
III. Series.
GV1794.C5718 2011
792.78—dc22
                                     2010004389

Editorial Credits
Jennifer Besel, editor; Strictly Spanish, translation services; Veronica Bianchini,
  set designer; Eric Manske and Danielle Ceminsky, designers;
  Marcie Spence, media researcher; Sarah Schuette, photo stylist;
  Marcy Morin, scheduler; Laura Manthe, production specialist

Photo Credits
All photos by Capstone Studio/Karon Dubke

**The Capstone Press Photo Studio thanks Dance Express in
Mankato, Minnesota, for their help with photo shoots for this book.**

Note to Parents and Teachers

The Baila, baila, baila/Dance, Dance, Dance series supports national physical education
standards and the national standards for learning and teaching dance in the arts. This book
describes and illustrates tap dancing in both English and Spanish. The images support early
readers in understanding the text. The repetition of words and phrases helps early readers learn
new words. This book also introduces early readers to subject-specific vocabulary words, which
are defined in the Glossary section. Early readers may need assistance to read some words and
to use the Table of Contents, Glossary, Internet Sites, and Index sections of the book.

Table of Contents

Tabla de contenidos

All about Tap

Make some noise with your feet! Move to the music with tap dance.

Todo sobre el tap

¡Haz ruido con tus pies! Muévete al ritmo de la música bailando tap.

Dancers use tap shoes

to stomp out beats

like a drummer.

Los bailarines usan zapatos de

tap para marcar el ritmo de

la música como un tambor.

is one thing... Dancing with the

Equipment

Tap shoes have metal pieces on the toes and heels. These pieces are called taps.

Equipo

Los zapatos de tap tienen piezas de metal en las puntas y los talones de los zapatos. Estas piezas se llaman *taps*.

Tap shoes make loud sounds against wood. Dancers practice in studios with wood floors.

Los zapatos de tap hacen un ruido fuerte contra la madera. Los bailarines practican en estudios con pisos de madera.

DANCING with the feet, is one thing... DANCING with th

Dancers wear costumes
during recitals. All costumes
let dancers move easily.

Los bailarines usan ropa de baile
durante los recitales. Toda la ropa
de baile permite que los bailarines
se muevan con facilidad.

Sweet Steps

Jump up and down on one foot. This move is called a hop.

Pasos dulces

Salta hacia arriba y abajo en un pie. Este movimiento se llama *hop*.

Strike your toes forward
on the floor. This move is
called a brush.

_____

Golpea las puntas hacia
delante en el piso. Este
movimiento se llama *brush*.

feet ... is one thing... DANCING with the Heart

Do the brush move with one foot.

Then slide that foot back.

This step is called a shuffle.

Haz el *brush* con un pie.

Luego desliza ese pie hacia atrás.

Este paso se llama *shuffle*.

Ready to Dance

Hop and shuffle to the beat.

Now you're tap dancing!

Listos para bailar

Haz *hops* y *shuffles* con la música.

¡Ahora estás bailando tap!

Glossary

beat—the rhythm of a piece of music

costume—clothes dancers wear during a recital

heel—the back part of your foot or shoe

practice—doing an action over and over to get better at a skill

recital—a show where people dance for others

strike—to hit with force

studio—a room or building where a dancer practices

Internet Sites

FactHound offers a safe, fun way to find Internet sites related to this book. All of the sites on FactHound have been researched by our staff.

Here's all you do:

Visit *www.facthound.com*

Type in this code: 9781429653534

Glosario

el estudio—un salón o edificio donde practican los bailarines

golpear—pegar con fuerza

practicar—realizar una acción una y otra vez para mejorar una habilidad

el recital—un espectáculo donde personas bailan para otras

la ropa de baile—prendas que los bailarines usan durante un recital

el talón—la parte de atrás de tu pie o zapato

el tiempo—el ritmo de una pieza de música

Sitios de Internet

FactHound brinda una forma segura y divertida de encontrar sitios de Internet relacionados con este libro. Todos los sitios en FactHound han sido investigados por nuestro personal.

Esto es todo lo que tienes que hacer:

Visita *www.facthound.com*

Ingresa este código: 9781429653534

23

Index

Índice